Instant Pot Electric Pressure Cooker Cookbook:

50 Instant Pot Recipes for Beginners, Healthy Instant Pot Recipes and Easy Instant Pot Recipes.

Wanda Carter

ISBN: 9781795638111

Table of contents

Introduction..6

Delicious Instant Pot Spaghetti...........................7

Sweet and Sour Chicken.......................................9

Yummy Chicken Rice Burrito Bowls...................11

Fluffy Potato Mashed.......................................13

Delicious Spicy Shredded Chicken.....................15

Asian Chicken Drumsticks................................17

Quick and Yummy Mac and Cheese...................19

Flavourful BBQ Ribs...21

Tasty and Easy Spanish rice..............................23

Garlic Cauliflower Mashed................................25

Almond Quinoa Porridge..................................27

Healthy Breakfast Oatmeal...............................29

Delicious Creamy Pumpkin Risotto...................31

Healthy Breakfast Quinoa.................................33

Sweet Cinnamon Apples...................................35

Herb Seasoned Chicken Breasts........................37

Classic Rice Pudding 39

Creamy Millet Breakfast Porridge 41

Delicious Roasted Potatoes with Bacon.............43

Easy Rice Pilaf 45

Easy Cilantro Lime Rice 47

Yummy Taco Chicken Chili 49

Delicious Spicy Taco Meat 51

Creamy Potato Corn Chowder.............................53

Buttery Chicken Wings 55

Healthy Lentil Curry 57

Quick and Spicy Paprika Rice 59

Creamy Green Pepper Chicken............................61

Yummy Sweet Potato Gratin 63

Easy Cheesy Parsnip Gratin 65

Coconut Pumpkin Soup..67

Delicious Potato Soup 69

Mix Vegetable Soup...71

Yummy Chicken Noodle Soup..............................73

Yummy Chocó Rice Pudding 75

Creamy Green Rice 77

Sweet Maple Glazed Carrots...............79

Instant Pot Potatoes 81

Cinnamon Apple Squash Mashed.......83

Warm Potato Onion Salad 85

Instant Pot Meatloaf...........................87

Simple Chicken White Bean Chili 89

Vanilla Banana Buckwheat Porridge.................91

Creamy Artichoke Spinach Dip..........93

Slow cooked Strawberry Breakfast Oatmeal.......95

Creamy Celery Coconut Soup.............97

Delicious Carrot Pea Soup...................99

Easy Potato Risotto 101

Tasty Carrot Shrimp Rice 103

Healthy Red Beans Rice 105

Introduction

Thank you for purchasing this book. This book contains 50 delicious and healthy Instant Pot Recipes. Instant Pot is electronic cooking appliance is specially invented to replace several kitchen appliances and making the yummiest, healthiest food in a safe, reliable and convenient way. This electronic appliance has 12 settings which you can be used for preparing your recipes and can be set according to the recipe. Instant Pot performs seven different functions in the kitchen. Slow cooker, Pressure cooker, Warmer, Rice cooker, Sauté cooker, Yogurt maker, Steamer. It is an all in one super-fast electronic cooking appliance. It reduces cooking time by being one it will do sautéing, boiling, simmering and browning. That means you spend less time in washing dishes. Instant Pot is made to be unitized on the top of the stove. A wellbeing valve, steam controller, and pressure actuated interlock instrument give security against the peril of blast and overheating. Also, Instant Pot uses 70% less energy to cooking your daily meals so that it saves your electricity bills.

Delicious Instant Pot Spaghetti

Total Time: 20 minutes

Serves: 6 Servings

Ingredients:

- 1 lb ground beef
- 2 tbsp extra virgin olive oil
- 8 oz spaghetti noodles
- 2 cups water
- 1 jar spaghetti sauce
- 1/4 cup onion, diced

Directions:

1. Add oil, garlic, and onion in Instant Pot and select sauté. Cook onion until softened.

2. Add ground beef and stir well and cook ground beef until all pink is gone.
3. Add water, noodles, and spaghetti sauce. Stir well.
4. Seal pot with lid and cook on manual high pressure for 7 minutes.
5. Release pressure using quick release method then open lid carefully.
6. Stir well and serve.

Nutritional Value (Amount per Serving):

- Calories 291
- Fat 10.2 g
- Carbohydrates 21.1 g
- Sugar 0 g
- Protein 27.3 g
- Cholesterol 95 mg

Sweet and Sour Chicken

Total Time: 20 minutes

Serves: 4 Servings

Ingredients:

- 16 oz chicken breast, skinless and boneless, cut into small pieces
- 4 tbsp water
- 2 tbsp cornstarch
- 1/2 tsp ground ginger
- 2 garlic cloves, minced
- 1 tbsp apple cider vinegar
- 2 tbsp ketchup
- 1/3 cup soy sauce
- 4 tbsp brown sugar

- 1/2 cup orange juice
- 1/4 cup water

Directions:

1. In a small bowl, combine together 1/4 cup water, orange juice, brown sugar, soy sauce, ketchup, apple cider vinegar, garlic, and ginger.
2. Place chicken into the Instant Pot.
3. Pour bowl mixture over the top of chicken.
4. Seal pot with lid and cook on manual high pressure for 5 minutes.
5. Release pressure using quick release method then open lid carefully.
6. Select sauté mode of Instant Pot.
7. In a small bowl, combine together cornstarch and 4 tbsp water and pour into the Instant Pot. Stir well.
8. Cook chicken on sauté mode for 2 minutes or until sauce thickens.
9. Serve hot and enjoy.

Nutritional Value (Amount per Serving):

- Calories 754
- Fat 26.5 g
- Carbohydrates 19.9 g
- Sugar 13.5 g
- Protein 101.8 g
- Cholesterol 300 mg

Yummy Chicken Rice Burrito Bowls

Total Time: 20 minutes

Serves: 4 Servings

Ingredients:

- 1 1/2 lbs chicken thighs, skinless and boneless, cut into pieces
- 2 cups chicken broth
- 1 cup chunky salsa
- 1 cup long grain rice, uncooked
- 15 oz can black beans, rinsed
- 1 tsp chili powder
- 1 garlic clove, minced
- 1 small onion, diced

- 1 tbsp olive oil
- 1/2 tsp salt

Directions:

1. Add oil, onion, and garlic in Instant Pot and select sauté mode.
2. Cook onion until soften about 2 minutes.
3. Add salt and chili powder and sauté for 1 minute.
4. Add chicken, salsa, rice, black beans, and broth and stir well to combine.
5. Seal pot with lid and cook on manual high pressure for 10 minutes.
6. Release pressure using quick release method then open lid carefully.
7. Stir well and serve with grated cheese.

Nutritional Value (Amount per Serving):

- Calories 667
- Fat 17.7 g
- Carbohydrates 62.6 g
- Sugar 4.0 g
- Protein 62.0 g
- Cholesterol 151 mg

Fluffy Potato Mashed

Total Time: 20 minutes

Serves: 5 Servings

Ingredients:

- 5 russet potatoes, peeled and diced
- 2 rosemary sprigs, chopped
- 3 tbsp butter
- 4 tbsp milk
- 2 garlic cloves, minced
- 3/4 cup vegetable broth
- Pepper
- Salt

Directions:

1. Add potatoes, broth, rosemary, and garlic in Instant Pot.
2. Seal pot with lid and cook on manual high pressure for 8 minutes.
3. Release pressure using quick release method then open lid carefully.
4. Using masher mash the potatoes until smooth and creamy.
5. Add butter and milk and stir well.
6. Season with pepper and salt.
7. Serve warm and enjoy.

Nutritional Value (Amount per Serving):

- Calories 222
- Fat 7.6 g
- Carbohydrates 34.6 g
- Sugar 3.1 g
- Protein 4.9 g
- Cholesterol 19 mg

Delicious Spicy Shredded Chicken

Total Time: 40 minutes

Serves: 6 Servings

Ingredients:

- 2 lbs chicken breasts, skinless and boneless
- 1/2 tsp oregano
- 1/2 tsp paprika
- 1 tsp garlic
- 1 tsp cumin
- 1 tbsp chili powder
- 14 oz can tomatoes, diced
- 4 tbsp brown sugar
- 1 can green chilies
- 1/2 cup chunky salsa

- 1 tbsp olive oil
- 1/2 tsp pepper
- 1/2 tsp salt

Directions:

1. Add chicken in Instant Pot and drizzle with olive oil.
2. Add remaining ingredients into the Instant Pot.
3. Seal pot with lid and cook on manual high pressure for 27 minutes.
4. Release pressure using quick release method then open lid carefully.
5. Using fork shred the chicken and serves with hot sauce.

Nutritional Value (Amount per Serving):

- Calories 357
- Fat 13.9 g
- Carbohydrates 11.9 g
- Sugar 8.9 g
- Protein 45.0 g
- Cholesterol 135 mg

Asian Chicken Drumsticks

Total Time: 25 minutes

Serves: 4 Servings

Ingredients:

- 8 chicken drumsticks
- 1/2 onion, chopped
- 1 tsp ginger, minced
- 2 garlic cloves, minced
- 2 tbsp rice wine vinegar
- 2 tbsp brown sugar
- 2 tbsp honey
- 1/2 cup soy sauce
- 1/4 cup water

Directions:

1. In a small bowl, combine together water, ginger, garlic, vinegar, brown sugar, honey, and soy sauce.
2. Place chicken drumsticks in Instant Pot then pour bowl mixture over the chicken.
3. Seal pot with lid and cook on manual high pressure for 10 minutes.
4. Allow it to release pressure naturally then open lid.
5. Now select sauté mode to reduce sauce.
6. Spray a baking tray with cooking spray.
7. Remove drumsticks from Instant Pot and place on prepared baking tray.
8. Broil chicken drumsticks for 2 minutes.
9. Once the sauce thickens, turn off the Instant Pot and pour sauce over drumsticks.
10. Serve hot and enjoy.

Nutritional Value (Amount per Serving):

- Calories 236
- Fat 5.3 g
- Carbohydrates 17.6 g
- Sugar 14.1 g
- Protein 27.6 g
- Cholesterol 81 mg

Quick and Yummy Mac and Cheese

Total Time: 10 minutes

Serves: 6 Servings

Ingredients:

- 1 lb elbow macaroni
- 1/2 cup parmesan cheese, grated
- 8 oz Monterey jack cheese, shredded
- 8 oz cheddar cheese, shredded
- 1 cup milk
- 2 tsp ground mustard
- 4 cups water
- 4 tbsp butter
- 1/2 tsp pepper
- 1/2 tsp salt

Directions:

1. Add water, macaroni, mustard, pepper, and salt in Instant Pot and stir well.
2. Seal pot with lid and cook on manual high pressure for minutes.
3. Release pressure using quick release method then open lid carefully.
4. Add milk, cheddar cheese, Monterey cheese, and parmesan cheese and stir well until creamy.
5. Serve hot and enjoy.

Nutritional Value (Amount per Serving):

- Calories 668
- Fat 34.0 g
- Carbohydrates 59.7 g
- Sugar 4.3 g
- Protein 30.2 g
- Cholesterol 97 mg

Flavourful BBQ Ribs

Total Time: 30 minutes

Serves: 6 Servings

Ingredients:

- 1/2 cup BBQ sauce
- 1 tsp garlic powder
- 1 tsp onion powder
- 1/2 tsp chipotle powder
- 3 lbs pork ribs rack
- 1 cup water

Directions:

1. Place steam rack into the Instant Pot and pour water into the Instant Pot.

2. Season pork ribs with onion, garlic, and chipotle powder and place on steamer rack inside the Instant Pot.
3. Seal pot with lid and cook on manual high pressure for 25 minutes.
4. Allow it to release pressure naturally then open lid.
5. Remove ribs from pot and place on baking tray and coat with BBQ sauce.
6. Broil pork ribs into the broiler for few minutes until sauce caramelized.
7. Serve and enjoy.

Nutritional Value (Amount per Serving):

- Calories 653
- Fat 40.2 g
- Carbohydrates 8.2 g
- Sugar 5.7 g
- Protein 60.2 g
- Cholesterol 234 mg

Tasty and Easy Spanish rice

Total Time: 25 minutes

Serves: 4 Servings

Ingredients:

- 1 cup rice, uncooked
- 1/2 tsp chili powder
- 1 red pepper, chopped
- 2 medium tomatoes, chopped
- 1 3/4 cups vegetable stock
- 3 tbsp tomato paste
- 1 medium onion, chopped
- 1/2 tsp pepper
- 1/2 tsp salt

Directions:

1. Add 1/2 cup broth, pepper, chili powder, and tomato paste into the Instant Pot. Stir until tomato paste is completely dissolved.
2. Add remaining vegetable stock and rice. Stir well.
3. Seal pot with lid and cook on manual high pressure for 10 minutes.
4. Release pressure using quick release method then open lid carefully.
5. Using fork fluff the rice and serve immediately.

Nutritional Value (Amount per Serving):

- Calories 212
- Fat 0.7 g
- Carbohydrates 46.8 g
- Sugar 5.8 g
- Protein 5.0 g
- Cholesterol 0 mg

Garlic Cauliflower Mashed

Total Time: 15 minutes

Serves: 4 Servings

Ingredients:

- 1 large head cauliflower, cut into florets
- 1/4 tsp garlic powder
- 1 tbsp butter
- 1 cup water
- 1/4 tsp pepper
- 1/4 tsp salt

Directions:

1. Place steamer rack into the Instant Pot and pour water into the Instant Pot.
2. Place cauliflower florets on steamer rack.

3. Seal pot with lid and cook on manual high pressure for 5 minutes.
4. Release pressure using quick release method then open lid carefully.
5. Drain cauliflower florets well and place in large bowl.
6. Add butter, garlic powder, pepper, and salt.
7. Using blender puree until smooth and creamy.
8. Stir well and serve.

Nutritional Value (Amount per Serving):

- Calories 51
- Fat 3.0 g
- Carbohydrates 5.5 g
- Sugar 2.4 g
- Protein 2.0 g
- Cholesterol 8 mg

Almond Quinoa Porridge

Total Time: 20 minutes

Serves: 4 Servings

Ingredients:

- 1 cup quinoa
- 1 tsp vanilla extract
- 1 tbsp coconut oil
- 3 tbsp honey
- 1 cup almond milk
- 1 cup water

Directions:

1. Add all ingredients into the Instant Pot and stir well.

2. Seal pot with lid and cook on manual high for 2 minutes.
3. Allow it to release pressure naturally then open lid.
4. Stir well and top with chopped almonds and serve.

Nutritional Value (Amount per Serving):

- Calories 375
- Fat 20.3 g
- Carbohydrates 43.7 g
- Sugar 15.1 g
- Protein 7.4 g
- Cholesterol 0 mg

Healthy Breakfast Oatmeal

Total Time: 20 minutes

Serves: 8 Servings

Ingredients:

- 2 cups steel cut oatmeal
- 1/2 cup walnuts, chopped
- 4 tbsp honey
- 1/4 tsp ground nutmeg
- 1 tsp ground cinnamon
- 1 tsp vanilla extract
- 2 ripe bananas, mashed
- 3 1/3 cups water
- 1/4 tsp salt

Directions:

1. Add all ingredients except walnuts and honey in Instant Pot and stir well.
2. Seal pot with lid and select porridge function for 10 minutes.
3. Allow it to release pressure naturally then open the lid.
4. Add chopped walnuts and honey and stir well.
5. Serve immediately and enjoy.

Nutritional Value (Amount per Serving):

- Calories 109
- Fat 4.7 g
- Carbohydrates 16.5 g
- Sugar 12.4 g
- Protein 2.2 g
- Cholesterol 0 mg

Delicious Creamy Pumpkin Risotto

Total Time: 20 minutes

Serves: 8 Servings

Ingredients:

- 3 cups pumpkin, diced
- 2 tbsp white wine
- 1 medium onion, chopped
- 2 garlic cloves, minced
- 2 cups Arborio rice
- 1 cup cream cheese
- 1 tsp sage, dried
- 3 tbsp extra virgin olive oil
- 4 cups vegetable broth

Directions:

1. Add oil, garlic, and onion in Instant Pot and select sauté mode. Sauté onion until softened.
2. Add pumpkin and sauté for another 1 minute.
3. Add white wine and sage, stir well.
4. Add rice and broth and stir well.
5. Seal pot with lid and cook on manual high pressure for 7 minutes.
6. After 7 minutes reduce pressure and cook for another 3 minutes.
7. Allow it to release pressure naturally then open lid.
8. Add cream cheese and stir well.
9. Serve warm and enjoy.

Nutritional Value (Amount per Serving):

- Calories 378
- Fat 16.6 g
- Carbohydrates 48.1 g
- Sugar 4.1 g
- Protein 9.0 g
- Cholesterol 32 mg

Healthy Breakfast Quinoa

Total Time: 10 minutes

Serves: 6 Servings

Ingredients:

- 1 1/2 cups quinoa, uncooked and rinsed
- 1/4 tsp ground cinnamon
- 1/2 tsp vanilla extract
- 2 tbsp maple syrup
- 2 1/4 cups water
- Pinch of salt

Directions:

1. Add all ingredients into the Instant Pot and stir to combine.
2. Seal pot with lid and cook on manual high pressure for 1 minute.

3. Turn off the Instant Pot and wait for 10 minutes.
4. Release pressure using quick release method then open lid carefully.
5. Stir well and serve with milk and chopped nuts.

Nutritional Value (Amount per Serving):

- Calories 175
- Fat 2.6 g
- Carbohydrates 31.9 g
- Sugar 4.0 g
- Protein 6.0 g
- Cholesterol 0 mg

Sweet Cinnamon Apples

Total Time: 10 minutes

Serves: 4 Servings

Ingredients:

- 3 medium apples, peel, core and sliced
- 1 tsp maple syrup
- 1 tbsp water
- 1 tsp ground cinnamon

Directions:

1. Add all ingredients into the Instant Pot and stir well.
2. Seal pot with lid and cook on manual high pressure for 2 minutes.
3. Release pressure using quick release method then open lid carefully.
4. Serve warm and enjoy.

Nutritional Value (Amount per Serving):

- Calories 93
- Fat 0.3 g
- Carbohydrates 24.7 g
- Sugar 18.4 g
- Protein 0.5 g
- Cholesterol 0 mg

Herb Seasoned Chicken Breasts

Total Time: 25 minutes

Serves: 4 Servings

Ingredients:

- 2 lbs chicken breasts, boneless
- 1 tbsp Dijon mustard
- 1 tsp sage, dried
- 1 tbsp rosemary, dried
- 1 tsp thyme, dried
- 1 tbsp honey
- 1 cup buttermilk
- 1 tsp pepper
- 1 tsp salt

Directions:

1. Add all ingredients into the large zip-lock bag and place bag in refrigerator for 1 hour.
2. Add chicken and marinade in Instant Pot and stir well.
3. Seal pot with lid and cook on manual high pressure for 15 minutes.
4. Allow it to release pressure naturally then open the lid.
5. Serve warm and enjoy.

Nutritional Value (Amount per Serving):

- Calories 479
- Fat 17.7 g
- Carbohydrates 8.6 g
- Sugar 7.3 g
- Protein 68.0 g
- Cholesterol 204 mg

Classic Rice Pudding

Total Time: 30 minutes

Serves: 4 Servings

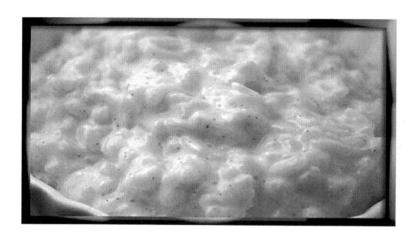

Ingredients:

- 1 cup rice, rinsed and drained
- 4 tbsp maple syrup
- 3/4 cup coconut cream
- 1 1/4 cups water
- 1/2 tsp vanilla
- 2 cups almond milk
- 1/4 tsp ground cinnamon
- Pinch of salt

Directions:

1. Add rice, salt, cinnamon, almond milk. vanilla, water, and maple syrup in Instant Pot. Stir well.
2. Seal pot with lid and select porridge function. It takes 20 minutes.
3. Allow it to release pressure naturally then open the lid.
4. Add vanilla and coconut cream and stir well to combine.
5. Serve warm and enjoy.

Nutritional Value (Amount per Serving):

*   Calories 602
*   Fat 39.7 g
*   Carbohydrates 59.7 g
*   Sugar 17.5 g
*   Protein 7.1 g
*   Cholesterol 0 mg

Creamy Millet Breakfast Porridge

Total Time: 20 minutes

Serves: 8 Servings

Ingredients:

- 2 cups millet flakes
- 1 tsp ground cinnamon
- 1 cup almond butter
- 1 tsp vanilla
- 1 tbsp coconut oil
- 3 tbsp maple syrup
- 2 cups heavy cream
- 1 cup water

Directions:

1. Add all ingredients into the Instant Pot and mix well.

2. Seal pot with lid and cook on manual high pressure for 2 minutes.
3. Allow it to release pressure naturally then open lid.
4. Stir well and serve with your choice of topping.

Nutritional Value (Amount per Serving):

- Calories 455
- Fat 21.4 g
- Carbohydrates 57.3 g
- Sugar 6.2 g
- Protein 8.8 g
- Cholesterol 55 mg

Delicious Roasted Potatoes with Bacon

Total Time: 15 minutes

Serves: 6 Servings

Ingredients:

- 2 lbs red potatoes, scrubbed and cut into 1 inch pieces
- 1/3 cup ranch dressing
- 4 oz cheddar cheese, shredded
- 1 tsp garlic powder
- 2 tsp parsley, dried
- 3 bacon strips, cut into pieces
- 1/2 tsp salt

Directions:

1. Add 2 tbsp water, bacon, potatoes, garlic powder, parsley, and salt in Instant Pot and mix well.
2. Seal pot with lid and cook on manual high pressure for 7 minutes.
3. Release pressure using quick release method then open lid carefully.
4. Add cheese and ranch dressing and stir well.
5. Serve hot and enjoy.

Nutritional Value (Amount per Serving):

- Calories 239
- Fat 10.5 g
- Carbohydrates 25.5 g
- Sugar 2.1 g
- Protein 11.3 g
- Cholesterol 30 mg

Easy Rice Pilaf

Total Time: 30 minutes

Serves: 6 Servings

Ingredients:

- 1 1/2 cups long grain rice
- 2 tbsp parsley, chopped
- 1 3/4 cups vegetable broth
- 2 garlic cloves, minced
- 1/2 cup onion, diced
- 2 tbsp butter
- 1/2 tsp salt

Directions:

1. Add butter in Instant Pot and select sauté mode.

2. Once butter is melted, add onion, garlic, and salt and sauté for 2 minutes.
3. Add rice and stir for 1 minute.
4. Add vegetable broth and stir well.
5. Seal pot with lid and select manual and set timer for 22 minutes.
6. Allow it to release pressure naturally then open the lid.
7. Using fork fluff the rice. Add parsley and stir well.
8. Serve immediately and enjoy.

Nutritional Value (Amount per Serving):

- Calories 220
- Fat 4.6 g
- Carbohydrates 38.5 g
- Sugar 0.7 g
- Protein 5.0 g
- Cholesterol 10 mg

Easy Cilantro Lime Rice

Total Time: 20 minutes

Serves: 3 Servings

Ingredients:

- 1 cup white rice, uncooked and rinsed
- 1 1/2 cups vegetable broth
- 1/4 cup fresh cilantro, chopped
- 1 lime zest
- 1 fresh lime juice
- Salt

Directions:

1. Add rice and vegetable broth in Instant Pot and stir well.
2. Seal pot with lid and cook on low for 12 minutes.

3. Release pressure using quick release method then open lid carefully.
4. Using fork fluff the rice.
5. Add lime zest, lime juice, salt, and cilantro. Stir well.
6. Serve warm and enjoy.

Nutritional Value (Amount per Serving):

- Calories 245
- Fat 1.1 g
- Carbohydrates 49.8 g
- Sugar 0 g
- Protein 6.9 g
- Cholesterol 0 mg

Yummy Taco Chicken Chili

Total Time: 35 minutes

Serves: 4 Servings

Ingredients:

- 1 1/2 lbs chicken breasts, skinless and boneless
- 1 oz ranch seasoning
- 1 oz taco seasoning
- 10 oz can tomatoes
- 16 oz can white chili beans

Directions:

1. Add all ingredients into the Instant Pot and mix well.
2. Seal pot with lid and cook for 30 minutes.
3. Release pressure using quick release method then open lid carefully.

4. Using for shred the chicken.
5. Stir well and serve.

Nutritional Value (Amount per Serving):

- Calories 354
- Fat 13.4 g
- Carbohydrates 4.7 g
- Sugar 2.4 g
- Protein 50.7 g
- Cholesterol 154 mg

Delicious Spicy Taco Meat

Total Time: 45 minutes

Serves: 8 Servings

Ingredients:

- 2 lbs ground beef
- 1/2 tsp chipotle powder
- 1/2 tsp cayenne
- 1 tsp cumin
- 1 tsp paprika
- 1/2 tsp pepper
- 1/2 tsp turmeric
- 1 tsp basil, dried
- 2 tsp oregano
- 2 tsp chili powder
- 5 garlic cloves, minced
- 3 green bell pepper, diced

- 2 medium onion, diced
- 4 tbsp olive oil
- 1 tsp salt

Directions:

1. Add all ingredients into the Instant Pot and mix well until combine.
2. Select sauté and sauté beef mixture for 5 minutes.
3. Seal pot with lid and select Bean/chili function. It takes 30 minutes.
4. Allow it to release pressure naturally then open the lid.
5. Stir well and serve.

Nutritional Value (Amount per Serving):

- Calories 305
- Fat 14.5 g
- Carbohydrates 7.7 g
- Sugar 3.6 g
- Protein 35.5 g
- Cholesterol 101 mg

Creamy Potato Corn Chowder

Total Time: 20 minutes

Serves: 6 Servings

Ingredients:

- 6 medium potatoes, diced
- 3 tbsp butter
- 2 tbsp cornstarch
- 3 cups half and half
- 3/4 cup cheddar cheese
- 3 cups chicken broth
- 1 small onion, diced
- 4 ears of corn, remove the kernels
- 1/8 tsp salt

Directions:

1. Add butter in Instant Pot and select sauté.

2. Once butter is melted, add onion and cook until softened.
3. Add corn, potatoes, salt, and broth. Stir well.
4. Seal pot with lid and cook on manual high pressure for 10 minutes.
5. Release pressure using quick release method then open lid carefully.
6. Combine together with a little water and cornstarch and pour into the Instant Pot. Stir well.
7. Select sauté mode and allow to mixture boil.
8. Add cheese and half and half. Stir well and cook until thickened.
9. Serve warm and enjoy.

Nutritional Value (Amount per Serving):

- Calories 534
- Fat 26.5 g
- Carbohydrates 62.2 g
- Sugar 6.9 g
- Protein 16.6 g
- Cholesterol 75 mg

Buttery Chicken Wings

Total Time: 15 minutes

Serves: 12 Servings

Ingredients:

- 3 lbs chicken wings, frozen
- 8 tbsp butter
- 1/2 cup water
- 1 cup hot sauce
- 1 oz ranch seasoning

Directions:

1. In a bowl, combine together hot sauce, butter, and ranch seasoning.
2. Add chicken wings into the Instant Pot.
3. Pour water and hot sauce mixture over the top of chicken wings.

4. Seal pot with lid and cook on manual high pressure for 12 minutes.
5. Release pressure using quick release method then open lid carefully.
6. Remove chicken wings from pot and place on baking tray.
7. Place in broiler and broil for 2 minutes.
8. Serve hot and enjoy.

Nutritional Value (Amount per Serving):

- Calories 285
- Fat 16.1 g
- Carbohydrates 0.4 g
- Sugar 0 g
- Protein 33.0 g
- Cholesterol 121 mg

Healthy Lentil Curry

Total Time: 25 minutes

Serves: 4 Servings

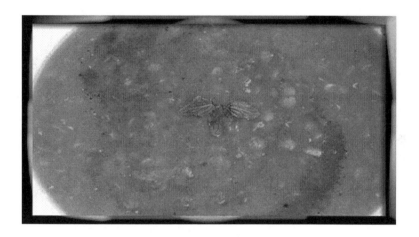

Ingredients:

- 1 1/2 cups lentils
- 2 cups vegetable broth
- 14 oz can tomatoes, diced
- 15 oz coconut milk
- 1/8 tsp ground ginger
- 2 tbsp red curry paste
- 3 garlic cloves, minced
- 1 large onion, diced

Directions:

1. Add splash of broth, onion, and garlic in Instant Pot and sauté onion until brown.

2. Once onion is lightly brown, turn off the sauté function.
3. Add ground ginger and red curry paste and stir well.
4. Add lentils, broth, tomatoes, and coconut milk. Stir well.
5. Seal pot with lid and select manual and reduce time to 6 minutes.
6. Allow it to release pressure naturally then open the lid.
7. Stir well and serve.

Nutritional Value (Amount per Serving):

- Calories 588
- Fat 29.1 g
- Carbohydrates 60.5 g
- Sugar 10.3 g
- Protein 24.9 g
- Cholesterol 0 mg

Quick and Spicy Paprika Rice

Total Time: 10 minutes

Serves: 6 Servings

Ingredients:

- 2 cups rice
- 2 cubes chicken bouillon
- 3 tsp paprika
- 2 1/2 cups vegetable broth
- 2 tbsp butter
- 1/4 tsp pepper
- 1 tsp salt

Directions:

1. Add all ingredients into the Instant Pot and stir well.

2. Seal pot with lid and cook on manual high pressure for 7 minutes.
3. Release pressure using quick release method then open lid carefully.
4. Using fork fluff the rice.
5. Serve warm and enjoy.

Nutritional Value (Amount per Serving):

- Calories 281
- Fat 5.1 g
- Carbohydrates 50.5 g
- Sugar 0.6 g
- Protein 6.8 g
- Cholesterol 10 mg

Creamy Green Pepper Chicken

Total Time: 15 minutes

Serves: 2 Servings

Ingredients:

- 8 oz chicken breasts, skinless and boneless, cut into pieces
- 2 tbsp garlic powder
- 1 medium onion, sliced
- 1 red pepper, sliced
- 1 green pepper, sliced
- 1/2 cup sour cream
- 2 cups chicken broth

Directions:

1. Add all ingredients into the Instant Pot and stir well.

2. Seal pot with lid and cook on manual high pressure for 8 minutes.
3. Allow it to release pressure naturally then open the lid.
4. Serve and enjoy.

Nutritional Value (Amount per Serving):

- Calories 458
- Fat 22.2 g
- Carbohydrates 21.9 g
- Sugar 9.6 g
- Protein 42.6 g
- Cholesterol 126 mg

Yummy Sweet Potato Gratin

Total Time: 20 minutes

Serves: 4 Servings

Ingredients:

- 4 sweet potato, sliced into coins
- 2 cups cheddar cheese
- 1 cup cream cheese
- 1 tbsp garlic powder
- 1 tsp chili powder
- 1 tbsp pepper
- 2 cups vegetable broth
- 2 garlic cloves, chopped
- 3 tbsp olive oil

Directions:

1. Add all ingredients except cheese into the Instant Pot.
2. Seal pot with lid and cook on manual high pressure for 4 minutes.
3. Allow it to release pressure naturally then open the lid.
4. Sprinkle cheddar cheese over the sweet potato mixture and select warm for 5 minutes.
5. Serve warm and enjoy.

Nutritional Value (Amount per Serving):

- Calories 658
- Fat 50.5 g
- Carbohydrates 29.8 g
- Sugar 8.8 g
- Protein 23.9 g
- Cholesterol 123 mg

Easy Cheesy Parsnip Gratin

Total Time: 20 minutes

Serves: 5 Servings

Ingredients:

- 5 cups parsnip, sliced
- 2 cups mozzarella cheese
- 1 cup cream cheese
- 1 tbsp garlic powder
- 1 tbsp pepper
- 2 cups vegetable broth
- 3 garlic cloves, minced
- 3 tbsp olive oil

Directions:

1. Add all ingredients into the Instant Pot, except cheese.

2. Seal pot with lid and cook on manual high pressure for 4 minutes.
3. Allow it to release pressure naturally then open the lid.
4. Sprinkle mozzarella cheese and select warm for 5 minutes.
5. Serve warm and enjoy.

Nutritional Value (Amount per Serving):

- Calories 393
- Fat 27.6 g
- Carbohydrates 28.6 g
- Sugar 7.2 g
- Protein 10.8 g
- Cholesterol 57 mg

Coconut Pumpkin Soup

Total Time: 25 minutes

Serves: 4 Servings

Ingredients:

- 3 cups pumpkin cubed
- 2 tbsp olive oil
- 1 tsp ginger powder
- 3 garlic cloves, chopped
- 1 medium onion, diced
- 1 cup coconut milk
- 3 cups vegetable broth
- 1 tsp pepper
- Pinch of salt

Directions:

1. Select sauté mode of Instant Pot.

2. Add oil, onion, garlic, and pumpkin and sauté until onion soften.
3. Add remaining ingredients into the Instant Pot and stir well.
4. Seal pot with lid and cook on manual high for 10 minutes.
5. Allow it to release pressure naturally then open the lid.
6. Using blender puree the soup until smooth and creamy.
7. Serve warm and enjoy.

Nutritional Value (Amount per Serving):

- Calories 307
- Fat 22.9 g
- Carbohydrates 22.8 g
- Sugar 9.8 g
- Protein 7.6 g
- Cholesterol 0 mg

Delicious Potato Soup

Total Time: 25 minutes

Serves: 4 Servings

Ingredients:

- 3 cups potatoes, cubed
- 3 cups chicken broth
- 1 medium carrot, diced
- 2 garlic cloves, chopped
- 1 medium onion, diced
- 1 tsp pepper
- Salt

Directions:

1. Select sauté mode and add oil, onion, garlic, and potatoes and sauté until onion soften.

2. Add remaining ingredients into the Instant Pot and stir well.
3. Seal pot with lid and cook on manual high pressure for 10 minutes.
4. Allow it to release pressure naturally then open the lid.
5. Using blender puree the soup until smooth.
6. Stir well and serve.

Nutritional Value (Amount per Serving):

- Calories 127
- Fat 1.2 g
- Carbohydrates 23.3 g
- Sugar 3.8 g
- Protein 6.1 g
- Cholesterol 0 mg

Mix Vegetable Soup

Total Time: 25 minutes

Serves: 4 Servings

Ingredients:

- 3 cups chicken broth
- 1/2 cup fennel, diced
- 1 cup celery stalk, diced
- 1 medium carrot, diced
- 2 potatoes, diced
- 1 tsp pepper
- 2 garlic cloves, chopped
- 1 medium onion, diced

Directions:

1. Add oil, onion, garlic, and potatoes in Instant Pot and select sauté until onion soften.

2. Add remaining ingredients into the pot and stir well.
3. Seal pot with lid and cook on manual high pressure for 10 minutes.
4. Allow it to release pressure naturally then open the lid.
5. Stir well and serve.

Nutritional Value (Amount per Serving):

- Calories 131
- Fat 1.3 g
- Carbohydrates 23.9 g
- Sugar 4.0 g
- Protein 6.3 g
- Cholesterol 0 mg

Yummy Chicken Noodle Soup

Total Time: 20 minutes

Serves: 4 Servings

Ingredients:

- 2 cups chicken, cut into pieces
- 1 cup noodles, broken into pieces
- 1 garlic clove, chopped
- 1 medium onion, chopped
- 1 medium potato, chopped
- 1 cup celery, chopped
- 5 cups chicken broth
- 1 tsp pepper

Directions:

1. Add all ingredients into the Instant Pot and stir well.

2. Seal pot with lid and cook on manual high pressure for 6 minutes.
3. Allow it to release pressure naturally then open the lid.
4. Stir well and serve.

Nutritional Value (Amount per Serving):

- Calories 267
- Fat 4.8 g
- Carbohydrates 24.4 g
- Sugar 3.0 g
- Protein 29.8 g
- Cholesterol 66 mg

Yummy Chocó Rice Pudding

Total Time: 30 minutes

Serves: 4 Servings

Ingredients:

- 2 eggs, beaten
- 1 tbsp coconut oil
- 1 cup coconut sugar
- 2 tbsp cocoa powder
- 1 tsp vanilla
- 5 cups coconut milk
- 1 cup rice, rinsed

Directions:

1. Add all ingredients into the Instant Pot and select sauté mode.
2. Stir continuously and bring to boil.

3. Seal pot with lid and select rice function.
4. Allow it to release pressure naturally then open the lid.
5. Stir well and serve.

Nutritional Value (Amount per Serving):

- Calories 929
- Fat 77.8 g
- Carbohydrates 55.4 g
- Sugar 10.4 g
- Protein 13.4 g
- Cholesterol 82 mg

Creamy Green Rice

Total Time: 25 minutes

Serves: 3 Servings

Ingredients:

- 1 cup rice
- 4 tbsp green hot sauce
- 1/2 cup fresh cilantro, chopped
- 1/2 avocado, flesh
- 1 1/4 cups vegetable broth
- Pepper
- Salt

Directions:

1. Add vegetable broth and rice in Instant Pot.

2. Seal pot with lid and cook on high for 3 minutes.
3. Allow release pressure naturally then open the lid.
4. Add green sauce, avocado and cilantro in a blender and blend until smooth.
5. Add avocado mixture in rice and mix well.
6. Season with pepper and salt.
7. Serve and enjoy.

Nutritional Value (Amount per Serving):

- Calories 310
- Fat 7.5 g
- Carbohydrates 52 g
- Sugar 0.6 g
- Protein 7 g
- Cholesterol 0 mg

Sweet Maple Glazed Carrots

Total Time: 15 minutes

Serves: 8 Servings

Ingredients:

- 2 lbs carrots, peeled and sliced
- 1 tbsp maple syrup
- 1 tbsp butter
- 1 cup water
- 4 tbsp raisins
- Pepper
- Salt

Directions:

1. Add water, carrots, and raisins in Instant Pot.
2. Seal pot with lid and cook on high pressure for 3 minutes.

3. Release pressure using the quick release method, then open lid carefully.
4. Drained carrot and place in bowl.
5. Add butter and maple syrup in a bowl and mix until butter is melted.
6. Season with pepper and salt.
7. Serve and enjoy.

Nutritional Value (Amount per Serving):

- Calories 80
- Fat 1.5 g
- Carbohydrates 16 g
- Sugar 9 g
- Protein 1 g
- Cholesterol 4 mg

Instant Pot Potatoes

Total Time: 20 minutes

Serves: 4 Servings

Ingredients:

- 1 1/2 lbs potatoes, cut into wedges
- 3 tbsp extra virgin olive oil
- 1 cup vegetable broth
- 1/4 tsp pepper
- 1/2 tsp onion powder
- 1/4 tsp paprika
- 1/2 tsp salt
- 1 tsp garlic powder

Directions:

1. Add oil in the Instant Pot and select sauté.

2. Add potatoes and sauté for 8 minutes.
3. Add onion powder, garlic powder, salt, paprika, black pepper and broth. Stir well.
4. Seal pot with lid and select manual low pressure for 7 minutes.
5. Release pressure using the quick release method than open the lid carefully.
6. Serve and enjoy.

Nutritional Value (Amount per Serving):

- Calories 221
- Fat 11.0 g
- Carbohydrates 27.8 g
- Sugar 2 g
- Protein 4 g
- Cholesterol 0 mg

Cinnamon Apple Squash Mashed

Total Time: 20 minutes

Serves: 4 Servings

Ingredients:

- 1 lb butternut squash, cut into 2 inch pieces
- 2 medium apples, cored and sliced
- 1/4 tsp cinnamon
- 1 onion, sliced
- 1/8 tsp ginger
- 1 cup water
- 2 tbsp oil
- 1/4 tsp salt

Directions:

1. Pour water into the Instant Pot and place steamer rack in the pot.
2. Combine together apples, onion and butternut squash and place on steamer rack. Season with salt.
3. Seal pot with lid and select manual high pressure for 8 minutes.
4. Release pressure using the quick release method, then open lid carefully.
5. Place apple and squash mixture into the bowl.
6. Using a masher, mash the apple and squash until smooth and creamy.
7. Add oil, cinnamon, and ginger in a bowl and mix until combined.
8. Serve and enjoy.

Nutritional Value (Amount per Serving):

- Calories 181
- Fat 7.1 g
- Saturated fat 1 g
- Carbohydrates 31 g
- Sugar 15 g
- Protein 1 g
- Cholesterol 0 mg

Warm Potato Onion Salad

Total Time: 20 minutes

Serves: 4 Servings

Ingredients:

- 1 1/2 lbs potatoes, diced
- 1 onion, chopped
- 1/4 cup parsley, chopped
- 2 tbsp olive oil
- 2 tbsp apple cider vinegar
- 1/2 tsp salt

Directions:

1. Place steamer rack in Instant Pot and pour 1 cup water.
2. Place potatoes on rack and seal pot with lid.
3. Select manual high pressure for 4 minutes.

4. Release pressure using the quick release method than open the lid.
5. In a bowl, combine together onion, vinegar, pepper, and salt.
6. Add potatoes and parsley in bowl and toss well.
7. Serve and enjoy.

Nutritional Value (Amount per Serving):

- Calories 189
- Fat 7.3 g
- Carbohydrates 29.0 g
- Sugar 2 g
- Protein 3 g
- Cholesterol 0 mg

Instant Pot Meatloaf

Total Time: 30 minutes

Serves: 6 Servings

Ingredients:

- 1 egg
- 1 lb ground beef
- 1/2 cup breadcrumbs
- 2 carrots, shredded
- 1/2 onion, shredded
- 1/4 tsp pepper
- 1/4 cup milk
- 1/2 tsp salt

Directions:

1. Add all ingredients in mixing bowl and mix well until combined.
2. Shape the mixture into a loaf about 6 inches thick to fit on steamer rack.
3. Pour 2 cups water into the Instant Pot and place trivet in the pot.
4. Place prepared loaf steamer rack on the trivet.
5. Seal pot with lid and select manual high pressure for 25 minutes.
6. Allow releasing pressure naturally then open the lid.
7. Remove steamer rack and spread ketchup over the top of the loaf.
8. Cut into the slices and serve.

Nutritional Value (Amount per Serving):

- Calories 204
- Fat 6.1 g
- Carbohydrates 10 g
- Sugar 2.5 g
- Protein 25 g
- Cholesterol 96 mg

Simple Chicken White Bean Chili

Total Time: 25 minutes

Serves: 8 Servings

Ingredients:

- 3 cups can white beans, drained
- 3 cups chicken breasts, boneless and diced
- 1 tsp paprika
- 1/4 tsp cayenne pepper
- 1/2 tbsp cumin
- 15 oz can tomatoes, diced
- 3 oz green chilies, diced
- 1 large onion, diced
- 2 cups chicken broth
- 1/2 tsp garlic powder

Directions:

1. Add all ingredients into the Instant Pot and stir well.
2. Seal pot with lid and cook on high pressure for 10 minutes.
3. Release pressure using quick release method the open the lid.
4. Stir well and serve.

Nutritional Value (Amount per Serving):

- Calories 418
- Fat 5.6 g
- Carbohydrates 58.2 g
- Sugar 8.8 g
- Protein 36.1 g
- Cholesterol 47 mg

Vanilla Banana Buckwheat Porridge

Total Time: 25 minutes

Serves: 2 Servings

Ingredients:

- 1/2 cup buckwheat groats, rinse
- 1/2 banana, sliced
- 1 1/2 cups milk
- 1/4 tsp vanilla
- 1/2 tsp ground cinnamon
- 2 tbsp raisins

Directions:

1. Add buckwheat in Instant Pot with vanilla, cinnamon, raisins, banana and milk.

2. Seal pot with lid and cook on high pressure for 5 minutes.
3. Allow it to release pressure naturally then open lid.
4. Serve and enjoy.

Nutritional Value (Amount per Serving):

- Calories 248
- Fat 4.8 g
- Carbohydrates 44.6 g
- Protein 10.4 g
- Sugar 18.1 g
- Cholesterol 15 mg

Creamy Artichoke Spinach Dip

Total Time: 15 minutes

Serves: 8 Servings

Ingredients:

- 10 oz spinach, frozen
- 15 oz can artichoke hearts
- 1/2 cup sour cream
- 1/2 cup vegetable broth
- 8 oz mozzarella cheese, shredded
- 14 oz parmesan cheese, shredded
- 1 tsp onion powder
- 2 garlic cloves
- 1/2 cup mayonnaise
- 8 oz cream cheese

Directions:

1. Add all ingredients except cheese into the Instant Pot and mix well.
2. Seal pot with lid and cook on high pressure for 5 minutes.
3. Release pressure using quick release method then open lid carefully.
4. Add cheese and stir until cheese melted.
5. Serve and enjoy.

Nutritional Value (Amount per Serving):

- Calories 455
- Fat 33.7 g
- Carbohydrates 12.2 g
- Protein 28.9 g
- Sugar 1.8 g
- Cholesterol 92 mg

Slow cooked Strawberry Breakfast Oatmeal

Total Time: 6 hours 10 minutes

Serves: 6 Servings

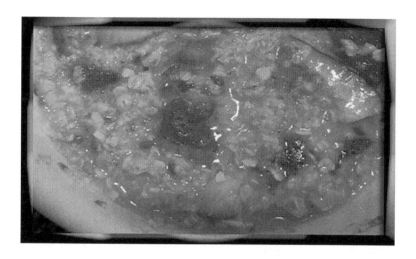

Ingredients:

- 1 cup fresh strawberries, chopped
- 2 cups oats
- 1 tbsp coconut oil
- 3 cups milk
- 3 tbsp honey
- 1 tbsp vanilla
- Pinch of salt

Directions:

1. Add all ingredients into the Instant Pot and mix well to combine.
2. Select slow cook function then cook on low for 6 hours.
3. Serve and enjoy.

Nutritional Value (Amount per Serving):

- Calories 230
- Fat 6.6 g
- Carbohydrates 35.2 g
- Protein 7.8 g
- Sugar 15.8 g
- Cholesterol 10 mg

Creamy Celery Coconut Soup

Total Time: 40 minutes

Serves: 4 Servings

Ingredients:

- 6 cups celery stalk, chopped
- 1/2 tsp dill
- 2 cups vegetable broth
- 1 medium onion, chopped
- 1 cup coconut milk
- 1/4 tsp salt

Directions:

1. Add all ingredients into the Instant Pot and stir well.
2. Seal pot with lid and select soup mode it takes 30 minutes.

3. Release pressure using quick release method then open lid carefully.
4. Puree the soup using blender until smooth and creamy.
5. Stir well and serve.

Nutritional Value (Amount per Serving):

- Calories 195
- Fat 15.5 g
- Carbohydrates 11.0 g
- Protein 5.5 g
- Sugar 5.6 g
- Cholesterol 0 mg

Delicious Carrot Pea Soup

Total Time: 40 minutes

Serves: 6 Servings

Ingredients:

- 1 lb split peas, dried
- 6 cups vegetable broth
- 2 tbsp salt free seasoning
- 1 onion, chopped
- 1 cup carrot, chopped
- 2 tsp paprika
- 1/2 tsp pepper

Directions:

1. Add all ingredients into the Instant Pot and stir well to combine.

2. Seal pot with lid and select bean mode, it takes 35 minutes.
3. Allow it to release pressure naturally then open lid.
4. Serve and enjoy.

Nutritional Value (Amount per Serving):

- Calories 272
- Fat 1.2 g
- Carbohydrates 49.9 g
- Protein 19.3 g
- Sugar 8.0 g
- Cholesterol 0 mg

Easy Potato Risotto

Total Time: 25 minutes

Serves: 4 Servings

Ingredients:

- 2 cups rice, uncooked
- 1 tbsp tomato paste
- 4 cups chicken stock
- 1 potato, cubed
- 4 tbsp white wine
- 1 medium onion, chopped
- 1 tbsp olive oil
- 1 tsp salt

Directions:

1. Add oil and onion in Instant Pot and select sauté for 4 minutes.
2. Add rice and stir for 2 minutes.
3. Add white wine and stir until rice absorbs wine.
4. Add chicken stock, potatoes, tomato paste and salt. Stir.
5. Seal pot with lid and cook on high pressure for 5 minutes.
6. Allow it to release pressure naturally then open the lid.
7. Serve and enjoy.

Nutritional Value (Amount per Serving):

- Calories 442
- Fat 4.5 g
- Carbohydrates 88.4 g
- Protein 8.0 g
- Sugar 2.3 g
- Cholesterol 0 mg

Tasty Carrot Shrimp Rice

Total Time: 25 minutes

Serves: 3 Servings

Ingredients:

- 1 egg
- 6 oz frozen shrimp, peeled
- 1 cup rice, rinsed and drained
- 2 tbsp soy sauce
- 3/4 cup frozen carrots and peas
- 2 garlic cloves, minced
- 1/4 tsp ground ginger
- 1/8 tsp cayenne pepper
- 2 cups water
- 1 small onion, chopped
- 1 1/2 tbsp olive oil
- Pepper

- Salt

Directions:

1. Heat 1 tbsp olive oil in Instant Pot.
2. Once oil is hot, add eggs and scramble them.
3. Transfer scramble egg from pot and set aside.
4. Add remaining oil with garlic and onion and sauté for 2 minutes.
5. Add carrots, peas, shrimp, rice, water, ginger, soy sauce, pepper and salt. Mix well.
6. Seal pot with lid and select high for 5 minutes.
7. Release pressure using quick release method then open the lid.
8. Add scramble egg and mix well.
9. Serve and enjoy.

Nutritional Value (Amount per Serving):

- Calories 392
- Fat 11.4 g
- Carbohydrates 52.7 g
- Sugar 1.3 g
- Protein 19.5 g
- Cholesterol 147 mg

Healthy Red Beans Rice

Total Time: 40 minutes

Serves: 5 Servings

Ingredients:

- 1/2 lb dry red kidney beans
- 5 cups rice, cooked
- 3 1/2 cups water
- 1 small bell pepper, diced
- 1 small onion, diced
- 1/4 tsp pepper
- 1 bay leaf
- 1/4 tsp dried thyme
- 2 garlic cloves, chopped
- 1 celery stalks, diced
- 1/2 tsp salt

Directions:

1. Add all ingredients except rice in Instant Pot and mix well to combine.
2. Seal pot with lid and cook on high pressure for 25 minutes.
3. Allow it to release pressure naturally then open lid.
4. Remove bay leaf from beans.
5. Serve with cooked rice and enjoy.

Nutritional Value (Amount per Serving):

- Calories 844
- Fat 1.8 g
- Carbohydrates 175.2 g
- Protein 23.9 g
- Sugar 3.0 g
- Cholesterol 0 mg

is the solitary and utter responsibility of the recipient reader. Under no circumstances will any legal responsibility or blame be held against the publisher for any reparation, damages, or monetary loss due to the information herein, either directly or indirectly.

Respective authors own all copyrights not held by the publisher.

The information herein is offered for informational purposes solely and is universal as so. The presentation of the information is without contract or any type of guarantee assurance.

The trademarks that are used are without any consent, and the publication of the trademark is without permission or backing by the trademark owner. All trademarks and brands within this book are for clarifying purposes only and are the owned by the owners themselves, not affiliated with this document.

38137029R00061

Made in the USA
Lexington, KY
03 May 2019